Shipping Container Homes

The Step-by-step Guide to Shipping Container Homes

(The Complete Guide to Understanding Shipping Container Homes)

Glenda Alfano

Published By **Regina Loviusher**

Glenda Alfano

All Rights Reserved

Shipping Container Homes: The Step-by-step Guide to Shipping Container Homes (The Complete Guide to Understanding Shipping Container Homes)

ISBN 978-1-7752672-2-5

No part of this guidebook shall be reproduced in any form without permission in writing from the publisher except in the case of brief quotations embodied in critical articles or reviews.

Legal & Disclaimer

The information contained in this ebook is not designed to replace or take the place of any form of medicine or professional medical advice. The information in this ebook has been provided for educational & entertainment purposes only.

The information contained in this book has been compiled from sources deemed reliable, and it is accurate to the best of the Author's knowledge; however, the Author cannot guarantee its accuracy and validity and cannot be held liable for any errors or omissions. Changes are periodically made to this book. You must consult your doctor or get professional medical advice before using any of the suggested remedies, techniques, or information in this book.

Upon using the information contained in this book, you agree to hold harmless the Author from and against any damages, costs, and expenses, including any legal fees potentially resulting from the application of any of the information provided by this guide. This disclaimer applies to any damages or injury caused by the use and application, whether directly or indirectly, of any advice or information presented, whether for breach of contract, tort, negligence, personal injury, criminal intent, or under any other cause of action.

You agree to accept all risks of using the information presented inside this book. You need to consult a professional medical practitioner in order to ensure you are both able and healthy enough to participate in this program.

Table Of Contents

Chapter 1: The Good And The Bad 1

Chapter 2: Designing Your Home 13

Chapter 3: Your Containers 34

Chapter 4: Crafting The Container 53

Chapter 5: Insulation 68

Chapter 6: Which Container Is Right? 78

Chapter 7: How You Can Protect Your Home From The Elements 104

Chapter 8: Types, Shipping Container Homes 125

Chapter 9: Site Preparations 158

Chapter 1: The Good And The Bad

There are pros, and cons, to owning and building any home. Be aware that there are pros and con's to every type of architecture. Shipping container homes are trendy and trendy, but you may end up paying more for a design than you intended or investing in something you don't love before you even get to move in.

Consider whether you want to build a tiny home with just one container or a bigger design that connects multiple containers together to create a larger living room. Standard shipping containers measure 40' in length. You can also get mini 20' containers, 45' high cubes or smaller 20' containers. The 20' shipping container is too small for most purposes, and the average volume of a regular container is 2377 cubic ft. Its equivalent size for a high cube container is 3026 cubic ft. Due to the fact that the high cube container can only be 8'10", you will need to insulate it, add pipes etc. below the floor. Unless you stack the 20' or standard containers, the height of a single home is not possible. However, these containers can be useful as "building blocks" when you add them to a modular-style home.

The Good

Prices

Shipping container homes often cost less than standard housing. They are much smaller than many duplexes and apartments but they still have their own internal space. Repurposing a container would make a home twice as big. The average used container cost less than $5000. Some even have ready-made kits or designs. A smaller 20" container can be bought for as low as $1400.

Insulate the container's top. Insulation is very important as it will prevent the container from becoming too hot in summer and too cold winter. There are three choices for insulation, with $0.30/ft2 being the cheapest. If you don't want your home looking like a shipping container it will also require some sort of insulation. It might seem odd, but people want their home resemble a home. However, in some areas, the zoning requirements require that the homes be disguised to blend in with local surroundings. These can be found at a cost of $2-3 per square ft.

A foundation is a necessary element of your home's structure. This will prevent the home's sitting on wet ground, and it will provide a platform. Concrete is relatively inexpensive and you can choose from three different methods. It is relatively inexpensive to buy a foundation for a 40-foot container. This foundation is not very attractive, but it can do the job if that is your goal.

These are just the basics.

While the average container home will cost $35,000 including the land, it can run as high as $50,000 to build a multi-container structure. It is not uncommon to find homes in desirable neighborhoods for less than this price. Even though you might find less expensive homes in bad or dangerous areas, if the house you desire is modern and well designed, it won't cost you as much. It will cost you approximately the same price as buying a small house with its interior already finished, but it will allow you to build your dream home for 2-3 times the amount.

The Time

Did you know that shipping container homes can be made in days?

Competant builders can build a simple house in less than seven days if they're not ordering something already constructed. Dependent on the design, many homes can take months or even years. Even though this is a professional turnaround it can still be completed quicker than a standard residence if you do the work yourself. You aren't required to hire licensed builders, architects or surveyors, since you're not actually building anything.

It is important to be able move into your new home in a short time. A majority of people won't be able move into an apartment so quickly. The idea of moving is appealing to those who like the flexibility of a shipping container home. They can be put on a truck and moved anywhere as long as there is a foundation and hook-ups. You would have to take your home down and unpack it. This way, you can keep your home exactly the way it is. It's possible to use a similar system for promotions, where the office/hub are simply boxed again and shipped wherever the company would like it.

Eco Considerations

This is a murky area. Some see the shipping homes as a great option for recycling defunct containers. Others lament the fact that they are the largest source of steel recycled and take away a resource that can be used better elsewhere. There is a large amount of unused or abandoned containers, especially along the coast. Many times, companies ship containers loaded with goods to the destination and then leave it there. Shipping the empty container back to the port costs more than buying a new container. There are thousands unused containers available, meaning there are many opportunities to purchase them. Many of these containers can be melted down into recycled steel. This produces carbon and other industrial chemicals.

Re-purposing a container "as it is" can help you reduce the environmental impact of recycling. It's also possible to reduce the carbon footprint by building an apartment building or a regular home instead of using containers. Reusing the container is a double-edged sword. You are reducing your carbon footprint as well stopping more contaminants, waste, and carbon from happening.

This is because the recycled steel actually is required. Many commercial and building processes require recycled steel in order to occur - such as equipment and buildings. If you take away this source, they will either be forced to buy new steel which may not be environmentally friendly or encouraged to use other methods.

Securer and Stronger

You've likely seen news videos after a tornado passes through. It's almost guaranteed that you will see shipping containers being carried around as toys. It's almost impossible to guarantee that shipping containers will be seen being thrown around as toys. A shipping container is much safer than traditional building in areas that are vulnerable to natural disasters. These containers can withstand hurricane force winds and the rough roads of global shipping. This makes them safer.

A traditional timber frame home looks very fragile. Since brick and mortar construction takes so long and is not as economically feasible to build, there has been a decline in the demand for them. For profits, building a house quickly and passing codes are all that is important. Older homes often survive centuries of natural disasters. Newer homes typically fall to the first cyclone.

What about simple theft. Standard homes have many windows and doors. A car can even pass through the wall. The shipping container is constructed of solid steel. This means that it won't allow you in and out. Also, the windows and doors you put in will be smaller than those you would find in a normal home. This makes it safer.

The Bad

It's Steel

Steel is not the preferred building material in most homes. Shipping containers were originally designed to be used for shipping goods. They usually have structural issues and are recycled after they have served their purpose. Although they are in perfect condition and can be reused, used containers can pose risks.

Containers get bumped around quite a bit over the course of their lives. They could be dropped, dragged around, dented, scratched or even banged in. Most people know steel rusts once it is exposed air and water, particularly seawater. This is because these containers are almost always near seawater and can rust. Even if rust is covered, it can cause structural problems and spread to other parts of the container. This problem can be solved by sandblasting the container, and then re-coating it.

Contaminants

Even though you may believe that you are doing the Earth a favor by reusing the container, you can't be sure of what you're exposing yourself to. Most containers are used in industry and can be subject to any number chemicals, not just lead-based. A container can be used to transport carcinogens (chemicals, toxins, biohazards) or anything else once it is used.

Containers are manufactured all around the world. One company might be already using recycled steel. You don't even know the exact conditions that this container was subjected to since its construction. This might have an effect on its integrity. Steel is strong and used for skyscrapers. However the container is fragile to extreme temperatures. The paint may also get scratched easily, making it difficult to clean. You'll need to drill into steel while building your home. This could release microparticles. If you live in the house for a long time, you may be exposed to compounds that can make you sick.

Weatherproofing

The outside of a metal or glass jar will sweat if you ever place something cold inside. Steel is a good conductor. It can transfer and hold heat well. This makes it extremely difficult to control the internal temperature of the container without adding insulation. It is not possible to keep all heat out of a container. Contrary to traditional construction, which creates several layers of barrier between you (and the outside environment), this design is not meant to be that way. This problem can be solved by insuring your home has enough insulation.

Chapter 2: Designing Your Home

France is home of some of France's most innovative and creative housing designs. There are numerous designs that can be used to create a livable space. Because a simple home is essentially an insulated brick box, there's not much design required. This is particularly true for prefabricated plans.

Prefabricated

Google will provide a range of prefabricated homes. These homes come with appliances and can come in various shapes and designs. They can cost anywhere from $21-40,000. Atomic Container Homes are the most well-known. Atomic Container Home's designs are simple and stackable. They look a lot like large construction companies' sites offices. However, they also have innovative designs with chic windows and other modern features. Atomic isn't cheap, but that's because they custom design your homes for you.

These units can also be purchased on ebay. The company offers designs that aren't in high demand with clients, or those that were created as sample units. Some of the designs are up to $300,000. Many of the ebay designs come pre-fabricated, ready-to-assemble and connected container homes. This includes a diagram, studs, all materials, and scrap materials. These materials can also be used as practice materials to help you remember the steps when you actually build your container home. The simplest kit cost $17895.

The company, which has been around for 20 years, is based in Scottsdale

Arizona. The company is supported by a team made up of architects and engineers, as well as their own construction company who will do the installation. You can visit their Texas facility to see how your home is being built. They use top brands like IKEA, 3M and others to ensure quality. If you don't have enough capital, you can get a mortgage similar to a regular residence. You have the option to purchase off-grid bunkers or bulletproofing. They also have three standard levels for build construction.

Prefabrication is similar to buying a regular house. You pick the company, select one of their plans, then they build it for yourself on your land. It's the easiest way to get a container-home and requires the least effort. However, it's also one of the most expensive.

Plans

The first step when creating your home, is designing it. The design stage is where you can map out the space and how it should look. Simple containers can be built by you figuring out the space, doors and hookups. More complex designs will require an architect. There are many companies who can design schematics for container homes. ContainerPlans is one company that excels at this task. ContainerPlans offers custom-designed plans as well as pre-made design layouts that can be purchased for as low as $10 per plan. These schematics will help your architect and construction crew see what you want.

They have a lot of plans, which is great for showing where everything will go. Their plans are not compatible with Atomic. They also don't include permits and any engineering work.

Plans

Here's a sample of how to design a shipping container.

The picture below shows how containers can be arranged inside and outside your home.

Codes for Building

Before you can build or buy anything, you should know the rules in your area. This includes land. Don't waste your money on land that is not zoned residential. And you won't be allowed to use it for shipping containers because it's against local rules. This applies to both pre-fabricated kits and constructions. The local government administration offices are the first to contact if you have plans to build. They will have a planning-and-zoning department, which is responsible to issue permits. If you've been considering land for a potential site, you should take this information and any plans or pictures. Even though it's most likely that you won't need this information, having examples of shipping container homes can really help. They will also have information about licenses, applications, and other pertinent information.

Some requirements may apply before you start. These can also increase the final cost for your home. You'll need to have soil tested, obtain easements from public property where your home will be located, and determine if you'll get rezoned if your property doesn't fit the criteria. These extra costs can vary from county to county so it is difficult to estimate.

Zoning

Zoning is the first. The local council defines what the land might be used for by zoning. This will often be displayed on boards for sale as letters - zoned C, F, R, etc. This doesn't mean that the land cannot be developed on in the way you desire. Or, you could be fined by the council and have to obtain pre-approval in order to build.

You should think about where buildings surround the land when you look at it. Are there neighbors who might object to your plans? How will the container home impact property values? Many large homes made from multiple containers have a modern appearance that can be combined with regular housing. However a design like the one in the above container may affect property values negatively and you might get denied. In the same way, land that is not zoned for agriculture and farming may be available to you if your plans are to build.

This information is usually obtained by either going online to search the local administrative office database or speaking to them in person. You can find out everything you need from the building department about your location and permits. Zoning laws may be complicated. It is important to check in person that your requirements have been set out.

Shipping container homes cannot be considered pre-feb homes.

Zoning is so important because it allows the government to make specific rules about how far away buildings should be and how much space must be left between the center of the road. Not the property owner, but the government. These are called Setbacks. It varies based on the structure and can prevent certain structures from being rezoned. Any construction must adhere to setback rules. All sides must be included.

New York has some of its most easy to understand laws. Zones R1-10 in the city are for residential areas. R1 zones tend to have the largest lots, and therefore are larger. R10 zones contain large apartment buildings, high-rises, and other structures that could be used for multifamily use. These are residential zones, and not commercial areas. Businesses that want to set-up or expand on these land parcels must get permits and potential approvals for rezoning. Construction takes place only inside the building.

Checklist:

It is important to get all the information you can about how your home will look and function before you purchase property. You can help by bringing construction plans and designs. There are not many laws that allow shipping containers in certain areas. More information is better because it shows that your work has been done properly and you have taken the time to research.

1. Contact your local county building administration to get started. Then, come in person with your plans and ask for information about the type of building you are interested in.

2. Multi-property considerations are a good idea as it is more likely that you can build alternative structures in rural areas than in residential areas, which could have financial implications. You might also reach out to the people living in the area and ask them if they are okay with you building there.

3. Ask about the Parcel Identifier. The PID will give you an idea of the zoning on the property, and whether it is suitable for construction. It will also allow you to discuss with the administration whether the property can be rezoned.

4. Ask about any zones or laws applicable to shipping container houses and not just pre-fabricated structures. This will verify that your shipping container can be used to construct a home or a modular home. Although it's possible for there to be a specific law here, do not be surprised if you are able

to get written confirmation that your shipping container has been approved.

5. Get the soil tested. This is the last step before buying. It will tell you if the soil can hold the container weight. Some soils may not be suitable for building work, or you might find that the area is a drainage ditch.

6. It is important to verify that any property you purchase is appropriate for your purpose and that it conforms to shipping container construction rules. You might lose money or face huge legal fees.

Where not to look for Property

Shipping containers can not be built in every area. This is mostly due mainly to climate. To make the project cost-effective, it is important to choose a cold or hot location because the containers can be difficult to insulate. It is evident that choosing a location with extreme cold temperatures will require both insulation inside and out, as well fewer windows to keep the boxes warm. This can lead to a dark interior. The same goes for desert areas. You will have to pay a high price just to keep it cool in both summer and the daytime.

For developing countries, basic shipping containers homes are temporary and can be inhabited when temperatures rise too much.

Avoid properties near water unless your goal is to construct a platform. Steel rusts. Any scrapes from construction or steel exposed could rust. If the trailer is situated on a flood plain your home may become inhabitable if it rusts.

Buying Land

You now need to be able to identify the exact parcel of land you wish to purchase. It is important to take a look at these things if your choice of rural location. Purchasing

Access Rights to Property

It might seem simple to purchase rural land in the middle or nowhere. However, if the land is not connected to the public road (road), then how can you expect to get there? You have two choices: purchase land to transport you from your land to the road, or negotiate an easement that allows to cross the boundary to reach the land of another. The rights to your land are not owned by you. This can be described in the following way: Your land is an "island", and the land surrounding it is an "ocean". Without a boat/bridge, it's impossible to get to it. You need to either rent the boat or buy it.

You can't force another landowner or owner to grant you access. Accessing land through another person is known as an "easement". This permits you to use their land for certain purposes without actually purchasing it. There may be additional conditions such maintaining the road or trimming hedges at your own expense. This must be in writing or the landowner will stop you from using the property. In your easement, include a clause that transfers rights to future heirs. This will ensure your property is protected in the event of an unforeseen event.

Do not assume an easement will be granted just for the sake of common sense. You will need an easement for cables, pipes and hookups that are required by law. There may be easements in place on the land where you plan to build.

Water

If you are building in a suburban location, it is likely that you will need to hook up with the local water and wastewater system just like any other construction. The plumbers can help you and the utilities companies will mark the pipes and arrange to provide service. In rural areas, well water systems and septic systems might be an option.

Florida recently received a case regarding a woman whose home was self-sufficient. The county condemned her home after she refused to make the connection, claiming that her rainwater collection was adequate. This seems extreme, but it's necessary in certain locations. Rainwater may not be collected where you live. Some states have laws that state the local government is the owner of all water rights. If this happens, you won't be able to use the water on your own land. This is something that you can also discuss at your local planning office.

If you plan on installing a well/septic, it is important to perform a dye testing. A dye test lets you know the drainage rate of the land. This is especially true if you have both a water source and a sewer system on the same parcel. To test for dye, you need to dig a hole and put water dyed with chemicals inside. If the water doesn't drain at the required rate, then the land won't drain well. This could lead to flooding in heavy weather. If the hole drains, you can see where the water comes from in the local water sources. You might find it in a creek just a short distance away or in the middle of a lake about a mile farther. There is no way to know where it will be, but local authorities won't issue permits for a sewer system without undergoing these tests.

Resources

You may think that your land purchase will make you the owner of everything within it, as well as all its contents. This is often incorrect. Every property, from minerals to oil to timber to air, has specific rights that will be set out in the deed. Mineral rights might not be something you think about, but the state may purchase you by compulsory purchase if they find oil there. They don't have to notify you, it's already in your deed. That means that you could come home to see your land being taken apart and a notice to tell you that it's not yours any more.

Similar, timber and trees located on your land are not yours. If the previous owner has negotiated a timber agreement that includes your land, this contract will hold regardless of whether you purchase the property. It's crucial to find out whether there is an existing contract, what timber they can take, from where, and how much. This can pose drainage problems as trees prevent flooding, and deforestation might make the land unsuitable to build on.

Pollution and Utilities

We have already talked about access easements. However, there are some things you can do to make sure your land is connected to the local public utilities. You should not assume the land is perfect.

This land was once used for chemical testing and spraying. It could also be dangerous to your health. While you may be allowed to drill a hole, you may not have power lines nearby. Solar and wind are great alternatives to traditional utilities. However there are often rules or permits that must also be followed.

You're seeing a lot of talk about pipelines in the news and their effect on the landscape. The DAPL is a prime example. Despite the fact the pipeline will not pass through Navajo lands, the nation is protesting it and many others. They are upset because, even though it doesn't pass through their land directly, it is near enough that a leak from the pipeline could potentially damage their land and destroy their livestock. Their land is not affected by the pipeline's proximity. The same applies to pesticides as crop spraying. While your land might not be directly sprayed by pesticides, the proximity could affect it. Remember Erin Brokovitch?

Protection

When you purchase an electronic from a shop, you are relying on two things: the store's returns policy and the manufacturer warranty. These two elements make it easier to buy the item, as you know that if something goes wrong, your money will be refunded. This step is often overlooked when buying land. Many people either don't even know that it exists or don't wish to spend the extra expense. Start by looking at comparable land and compare the price to other properties in the area. If the price is unusually high or low, it could be an indication that there are reasons for the extra cost. In order to protect your funds and get it back in case of problems, you will need an Escrow. As a topography chart can only tell you so far, there might be rocks that will hinder construction and leveling.

The majority of people skip title insurance. However they don't always have the correct document or the latest documents. There is a lot to be aware of, and a lot more legal jargon. This can make it overwhelming. Together, title insurance and Escrow will guarantee that your money goes only to the seller when the transaction goes smoothly. This is essential when buying land. It provides all of the information you need and also gives you the PID so you can work with local authorities or utilities.

Chapter 3: Your Containers

The beginning of the book was devoted to the different shapes and types containers. Although it is easy to see that these containers are made of large steel boxes, The standard sizes are 20, 40, 45 foot containers. They come in either a standard height (High Cube) or a higher height (Standard Height). This allows you to add inside pipes and insulation which will quickly take up space. These numbers are not exact because manufacturers typically allow for tolerances of +-5mm.

Many types of containers are available in port areas. But, they may not be readily available locally. Your budget might be more important than the items you actually want.

The first decision that you will make is whether or not you want to purchase a new container. One-trip containers were only used once before being sold.

They are generally not subject to a lot damage and have never been damaged. However, they will be more expensive if they are used. This will ensure that they last for a longer time than those that are marked as used. Additionally, it will lower the likelihood of your container being treated with chemicals and pesticides.

Inspection of the Container

Never buy a container unless you have seen it in person. Make sure to inspect each container before you purchase it. You can identify this code by looking inside the container. These numbers are an 11-digit number stamped onto the container. This number has a very specific makeup. It allows you track the containers journey and to determine whether the company is telling you the truth about the containers being used, new, or only one trip. The first three letters in the number indicate the owner. The fourth letter indicates the product. This is usually a U. Z. or J. U denotes shipping container, while Z denotes a trailer. Equipment attached such a refrigerator unit is J. You will see a six-digit serial number and a checkdigit at the bottom that mark a complete number. It should look like the following:

Begin by looking for scars and scratches, dents, spots and rust markings. You should inspect any areas that appear to be repainted. If there is information, ask about the previous cargo. If you find anything that appears to be damaged, you might get a discounted. However, it can affect the lifespan or structure of your home. You can save money by purchasing all of your containers from the same company. This will ensure that they are identical in size.

Where to Buy

Dealers are the easiest way to buy your container. These are not only available in the ports, but all over the country. Green Cube Network offers an easy way to find information about shipping container recycling. But a Google search can give you many other options. Reputable dealers offer the best solution for most people as they have a guarantee that other methods will not.

Online

Although you can purchase the containers online, it is unlikely that the container will arrive in person. There are many reliable sellers online, but it is risky because you can't guarantee you get the exact same container that was pictured. Alibaba, Gumtree and Ebay all offer the ability to search and purchase containers.

You can shop online for convenience, but it's important to look at reviews and reputations to see if the product is authentic. This is not to mention the fact that once you're inside a container, those numbers aren't really accurate measurements and it's much more difficult to determine how much space there is. Another problem when buying online, especially with Alibaba is that some containers are not local. You'll have to pay shipping charges. It's extremely expensive. That is why so many containers are "one-way", for example, shipping a container from China to the US could cost as much as $23,000.

Direct

It's not a good idea buying containers direct as most companies won't sell more than one or two containers. If you can find a company willing only to sell a few containers, it is more likely that they will charge you more than a dealer. This is because the dealer has a better deal for buying bulk. Dealers and distributors deal only with containers. They can obtain them from multiple sources. Companies will not sell directly to the general public.

You can search the internet or use the yellow book to locate companies. If you have trouble finding anyone, try calling a company not in your local area. They may know of distributors or dealers that might be available or who are willing to work with local customers. They may also sell containers.

Prices

Once you've purchased your container, you'll need a delivery time. The distributors and docks do not like this so be ready for a short delivery time. It's important that the ground be prepared before everything can be set up so that it can be installed as soon it arrives.

Preparing the land

Before you place your container, prepare a foundation. This will provide a stable, level platform for the container to stand on. Each type of foundation is acceptable, but not all local authorities accept them all. Therefore, you may have to choose one. It is best to have a qualified engineer and expert lay your foundations. This will allow them to be more familiar with the soil, codes, and topography of the area. Pile foundations, raft foundations, and concrete-pier foundations are all common for container homes. This is an area you should not compare the shipping container to a portable home.

Foundations

The cost and the structure of your foundation are two important aspects. Structurally, you should consult a professional because they will be able to advise on how to distribute the weight of your container. The foundation must be deeper for more stability. For hard soils or rocks, only minor foundation work is required. Over-specifying foundations is another way to increase strength.

Concrete Piers

These foundations can be used to support small sheds and outbuildings. These are concrete piers that contain reinforced steel beams and are strategically placed. The concrete's stability and strength is enhanced by the addition of steel bars and steel mesh. DIYing the foundation is the easiest method. It involves the least amount of concrete and the most scientific approach. These piers must be placed in areas where the "load" or main-weight of the containers is, i.e. the middle and corners. For more support, it is a good idea to add additional piers to the seams of multiple containers. It is normal to have six piers in each container.

Slab-on-Grade

Raft foundation can be more expensive than piers. However, it's much more stable and sturdy than piers. However, you will have to dig into the top of the soil. It's still very easy to build the raft foundation. This also means that concrete is more susceptible to cold and allows heat to leach from your container. This will make it less suitable for cold climates. The slab is also less susceptible to termites, bugs, and other pests because it doesn't have any wood. It is important to ensure your utilities are properly embedded in the slab. You also need to make sure the connections are connected to the containers. There will be no access to your utilities once the concrete has set.

Pile Foundation

These foundations are similar to concrete-piers. They are also deeper and more complicated, which is why these tend to be the most pricey. This foundation is used when soil is too weak or not suitable for a concrete slab. Graceville Container Home Study provides a great example of container home design. This study focuses on a family whose house was damaged by flooding. Their home, which was three-layered and measured 6000ft in length, featured everything you could need from a gym to an office. Because of flood and cyclone danger, they needed to have deeper piles.

Piles are made of steel tubes that are round and hammered to make them more solid. After they are secured, they will be filled with concrete rebar and steel rebar. It is the same material as the piers that are above ground. This construction cannot be done by yourself because you will need to hire a pile driver. This foundation is considered the strongest, and it is recommended that you use it even if you're doing multiple stacked designs.

Strip Foundation

It is rarer to find a mixture of slabs or piers known as strip Foundations. These are concrete strips with thick foundations that are laid on or around the container footprint. This is a less expensive alternative to a slab and more stable than the piers. Because the inside area is larger, this is a good choice in areas where the ground is wetter. They are however less stable than pile foundations and can slip in high winds, earthquakes or high winds. They are too shallow to be used in stacked container designs.

Concrete

Concrete is available in many different grades. For foundation building, you will need to use concrete with the right strength according to your land. The strength is measured using C and a number. Stronger concrete will be stronger. C15 is a general purpose concrete. C30, however, is a stronger concrete. C15 requires 1 part cement to 2 pieces of sand. 5 gravel is used. Concrete strength increases with the addition of cement. Although small quantities can be mixed by hand, you will need to have a mixer or order ready-mixed concrete. Although it increases the cost for your concrete, this ensures you don't get one piece of concrete already dried while mixing it. Mix it correctly so it is well combined. If it isn't, it can result in different structural densities. These could lead to cracks and weakness.

It is very easy to calculate how much concrete is needed. To do this, first determine how many square feet of concrete your concrete area covers. Then mix the concrete accordingly. For example, if you had a 20" container and a foundation that was only 2 feet in depth, then you would need to mix 10x22x2' concrete or 440 cubed feet.

Once the concrete has been mixed, it undergoes a curing procedure that eventually hardens it and sets it. This takes anywhere from 5-7 days. Some moisture should be added to prevent the concrete from drying out and cracking too quickly. The weather and temperature must remain relatively constant during curing. Extreme hot or cold temperatures can impact the curing process.

You'll need some shade to protect your concrete from direct sunlight in hot weather. Mix concrete with cold water and place it in the afternoon or early morning to avoid heat.

Cold weather: Clear away any standing water and frost from the foundation. Cover the concrete with an insulation blanket layer. The blankets should stay on for the entire curing process.

Footings

Footings will be needed within the concrete. These are required to support the foundation so it doesn't settle unevenly or crack. These are the "feet", or foundation feet, and they are usually between 16-20 inches in size. These work well in well-distributed soil.

However you may need to add different footings to your foundation to keep it solid. If the ground is uneven or not centered correctly, the weight above will push down on the foundation and cause the footings to shift. This can eventually lead to the foundation cracking. This is nearly always determined by engineers. Even they sometimes do it wrong. The bearing capacity of the soil and the type of soil determines how strong the footings will be.

Footings should be placed no more than 6 inches from the frost line. A footing placed above the frost line will shift with temperature changes as the earth freezes. This is crucial if you intend to use a shallow foundation. The National Snow and Ice Data Center contains information on your geographical frost line. These include the ground parameters and soil classes.

There are three sizes for an average footing, plus the frost line depth:

* 8" x 16' x 16".

* 12"x24" x24"

* 10"x20", x20"

Each footing is made separately. For example, if the design calls for leveling of a slope then you will start with those higher. Footings are made of 1/2" rebar. This is 8 times the thickness of the concrete. Once the hole is dug, the bar is driven or hammered to the ground. The rebar's top should meet the concrete's. The number of feet you have will affect the placement of the rebar.

This table applies to standard construction. However, it will also give you an idea about the expected bearing of each feeting if they are compared with the heavyest. Sometimes footings are not perfect. If the soil is not right, it may not be a problem. However if the foundation is not properly centered, it will need fixing using gravel, an additional tie steel or re-augmenting.

You might have a soft area, such as a spot where the concrete rebar is not visible. If this happens, excavate the soil and build a pile to support it. It is possible to remove the soft soil completely, and fill in the hole with gravel. It's not possible to simply increase the footing width without increasing the thickness. This can lead to concrete cracking.

The truth is that there's so much potential to be right about footings, it could even fill a book.

Fixing the Container

It doesn't matter which foundation you choose, you need a strong way to attach your container. A steel plate can be attached to concrete before it has cured. The steel plate should be able to sink into the concrete, adding stability.

After curing is completed, the container may be welded directly onto the steel plates. The plates should measure at most 1/4" to 1/2". Thicker plates tend to be stronger. You will still see a top of the plates and this should be level across all foundations. This applies to metal plates as well as attachment screws. If you're interested in DIYing, it's worth looking into the local codes.

Bolting the container directly into the concrete is an alternative to welding plates. This is much easier and cheaper but not as strong. J hooks may also be used for attaching the container to exposed concrete rebar. Concrete anchors are the weakest option but can be an added safety feature if you do this and plate welding.

There is no rule that says you must fix the container to your foundation. But, if there are plans to move the container at some point in the future you can choose to not. You can place the container directly on top of the foundation. But, it does not mean that the container will be stable. It may also affect your home insurer if the foundation is damaged. If you want your home to be mobile, it will be much harder for containers to be removed if they are welded.

Chapter 4: Crafting The Container

If you're building a simple home from one container, then you should look at insulation. Other times you will need knowledge about fitting multiple containers together. This is not all. How do you transform a steel box into a comfortable home? This must be more than just adding a couch. Even if your container only serves a temporary purpose, you must make sure it is properly insulated.

Connecting containers

The containers should be from the exact same manufacturer. Although you can connect containers made by other manufacturers, there's more risk. The local building department will require that you either follow the plan or stop any further building work. You can either purchase container joining tools or do it yourself.

The construction of containers is key to assembling them. A container can be described as a "unibody" design. This means it is made up of around 15 components that all work together in a single container. It's very efficient from an engineering point of view.

Stacking. Clustering. Or both

Your design might dictate that you stack your containers above each other. Shipping containers are designed to stack up at 10 inches without additional reinforcement. You can remove or adjust any doors, shape, or other elements from the container. However, once it's modified in engineering it changes its strength. Some things are impossible.

One container can only be designed for one purpose and is therefore not practical for most families. A modular design, which combines multiple containers into one container, is the best way to maximize the space.

The normal use of containers is to stack them and make sure they can withstand hurricane force wind. Standard containers in use will help you understand the rules of stacking. You need to make sure that the design is even and that the load is distributed correctly. Most containers stack directly on top. Although it may look boxy, this container is extremely strong and useful. Containers should only be stacked like they were intended. A smaller container cannot be stacked on top or beneath a larger container. This is because the corrugated iron on top of the container has a rating of only basic maintenance or the weight a human walking across it, not another container, and not more than 200kg. Containers are stacked by the load bearing beams, which align with each other. If the load is not evenly distributed, it can cause the containers to buckle.

You cannot place a container in another way. The bottom container is often nearly flat. It's almost as if the bottom one were your home.

You should never stack containers unmodified without adding support!

You have probably seen containers with the higher container facing forward than the lower one, or the upper container at an angle. Modifications are required for irregular stacking to distribute the load. This stacking is very complex, and requires a structural engineering engineer. This is because many designs are unique and can only ever be configured by an engineer or architect.

These containers do not conform to the rule as shown in the image above. Additionally, you will see yellow-painted I beams in the bottom layer that are part the structural reinforcement. The beams also serve to support the third level. These 22 containers will not stand on their own weight and require reinforcement. All containers must be reinforced. You will need to spend a lot if you want an unusual look.

A stack of two containers on top each other is the most practical and cost-effective design. Side-by side is equally efficient than trying to connect in any other manner.

It's not always easy to place containers side-by side. Because ISO corners have protruding fittings, this creates a gap between them. The gap is obviously a problem and it is quite difficult to fill. It's best to use inverted angle metal between the roofs and flat steel on the sides and floors. Because the container roof has a slightly angled roof, you don't want water to enter the joint between the containers. This creates a trap for water, which can lead to structural and corrosion problems.

Backer Rod is an alternative to joining the containers side by side. This soft material can be pushed in the jam like Play Doh then covered up. The Backer Rod inserts directly into the gap between both containers.

Many containers don't have the same dimensions. This is especially true when it comes to floors.

Interior Considerations

Modifying a container frame must be strong enough and secure enough to ensure it doesn't break when it is lifted onto the slab. The greatest threat to a home's stability is its ability to be lifted and moved. Many homeowners choose not modify the containers after they are placed. You may have to modify containers to stack them. Modifying stacked containers requires an engineer. It is not possible to modify clustered containers side-by sides without an engineer.

Side Wall Modification

Sidewall panels are not designed to be modified. This can affect the structure's load capacity. Because of the flexibility in design, there isn't much to test. Modifications should only be attempted with extreme caution. The sidewall's metal panels are made up of 11 separate pieces. They expand and contract with the weather. You can change the forces of the wall by removing a section. Other times, you may need extra reinforcement while cutting the container roof. This can create memory. The side walls are made out of 1.6mm Corrugated Steel. It is very heavy so you should be careful when moving it.

The roof can be removed safely from any side wall up to 8-10ft. However, extra reinforcement is advised to ensure longevity. Structural support is needed for roofs that exceed 10 feet. This is especially important when stacking. The extra weight can cause a weakness in the roof that can cave under the weight. To help support structural support, doors should have a minimum of 8 inches from the ceiling to reach the top of their doors. This is especially important in containers without side beams. You may also need reinforcement for roof. If there is no thick steel bar around the outside of the container, it will be obvious. If there is, it will provide some support. This bar creates the same shapes as steel, but is less expensive to make and has been used less by companies.

After the internal wall has already been cut, it will need grinding to get the edges even and then welding to the other container. It is important to make sure the edges are smooth and clean. A simple steel disc cutter works well. To seal the container gap below the floor level, you'll need a strip approximately

2" in width. This strip is not structural and will leave a slight gap at the floor. However, you should conceal this once you have laid your flooring. Expanding foam is great for filling in any gaps on the sides. The external edges should be welded or joined using Backer Rod. While the wall cures, you might want to secure the wall by clamping it together.

Windows and Doors

It is similar to sidewall modification in that you can cut window holes. However, this could affect the structural integrity of the structure and may require reinforcement. Stiffening around the window or door holes will prevent them from warping or being bent is the easiest way to accomplish this. Additionally, you'll need to find a way to attach standard window and door frames. This can be done easily by making a steel box frame that you then attach to the container. This gives you reinforcement and something that you can work into. It is comparable with wooden designs.

Windows are known for having low insulation values, so this should be taken into consideration. It is similar to internal modifications. To add windows or doors, you will have to grind it down, strengthen it, and weld a frame if needed. Cube Depot also specializes on modifications for container-homes. Standard windows can only be basic frames. They would typically fit into wooden framing, and then be screwed. It's possible to still do this but you will need to attach them a metal framework and seal the gaps to keep moisture out. This will allow drips to be prevented from entering the frame through the window.

It is possible to place windows in a strategic way. These should always be taken into consideration during construction and should be established before the start of construction.

Because this could affect where you want windows, it is important to consider the interior layout. There may be building codes that govern the size or number of windows. You should check this information during the planning process. You might need to redesign your home if certain authorities insist on a certain number or amount of windows.

Skylights are also an option if your containers don't have to be stacked. They can affect structural integrity but should not be heavy and cannot drain water away. If you have standing water or mold, this could cause steel to rust. These skylights provide natural light for areas within your container that aren't suitable for windows. Some skylights won't work well in containers.

You'll need a door for the home. However, most people do not choose to use the standard latch doors provided with the container. They prefer to use the steel elsewhere. This leaves an unfilled space that will need filling. There are many options. Most people choose rolling or traditional doors. For security, you should consider a lockbox or a welded section in the frame. This will prevent the door from being kicked in.

Roll up

Rollup doors are similar in size to electric garages and can measure between 4-10ft. They can be equipped with sliding clasp locks. They can also be made of galvanized steel 26 inches in length or aluminum 26 inches in width. These look more industrial.

First, you need to place the rails. Measure the door to ensure there is enough space between the rails. To attach the rails, you should snap lines into the container wall at exactly the right height so that the rails can be fitted in. After grinding the surface, attach the rails to the wall. Mark the container on top where the bolt holes for the rail are so that you know where to weld. Finally, take off any paint and grind it off to create a clean welding area. Attach the rails to the wall by clamping them and then tack welding the rails in place. Check the door to make sure it has the correct orientation. Attach the door with bolts to the top wall, above the rails. But don't tighten them down until it is perfectly in place. You will need to push the door down against the container. Next, tighten the screws and then bend the tabs slightly so the door can drop in. Remove the banding from the door before you release it. Take a look at the rails from above. You should be able to see the door at the bottom of the hole. Before welding the rails correctly, roll the door again. Also, weld where the bolts for your door are.

The door has been attached. Now you need to adjust its spring tension and attach the hardware. The large nut located at the end bar where the door rolls is used to adjust the spring tension. Turn the nut to open and close the door slightly before attaching the brackets. The door should be tensioned until it rolls upwards at the halfway point. It should then roll down without any assistance. It should feel like a pull-up motion when it is not held down.

Rollup doors usually come with instructions. Make sure you follow them, especially if there is additional hardware.

Insulation will be the biggest challenge when installing a rollup garage door. It is not possible to use traditional methods and it will also make your home look ugly.

Traditional Door

Most traditional residential doors made from wood are wooden. All-steel doors can be found, but they are more expensive. The average dimensions are 3 feet wide, 7 feet high, and approximately 3 feet long. These can be attached as windows, with a steel frame being welded into a container wall. Once the steel frame has been cut out, it is bolted to the wall. This is the best option. The wall will not be cut too much. It allows you to place windows on the side of the door to maximize the available space.

Chapter 5: Insulation

Insulation is mandatory for all containers. It's impossible to avoid this. But, it is possible to have your container insulated differently depending on where you will be living. Insulation generally comes with two ratings - R or U. Insulation is usually classified with two ratings: R and U. The R value measures the resistance of the material for temperature changes. Insulators with higher R numbers are more efficient. The U value represents the opposite. It is the amount of heat that is lost using various methods. The less efficient and less insulating material is, the higher its U value. Insulation materials that are most commonly used in buildings include panels, blankets batts, and fiberglass. But container homes also permit for expanding or spray foam insulation. The R value of the container has 0.33 while fiberglass has 3.14. You can see why it should be insulated.

There are many different materials available, but you will need to verify that the building codes are being followed.

Framing of the container

Framing is necessary to attach your insulation inside the container. This same method is used in standard construction. The pockets are where insulation is attached. Finally, paneling is added. This is especially important if the climate is cold. It is important to first close all holes. This is actually very simple but you must be precise. Make 2'x4's space 2' from floor to ceiling. Cover any windows or doors with this framing. You should attach the frame directly to your container. Before installing insulation, you need to add wiring, pipe and other plumbing. Your frame should extend several inches beyond your container. This allows you to place pipes and wires in the best space.

Once the framing material is installed, fill the area with your choice of insulation. Add panels on top. Make sure to cut holes for any water pipes or electronic fixtures.

Fiberglass

Fiberglass insulation comes as rolls of approximately 2 feet long and costs about $40. They

The ratings range from R10-30. You can select any scale according to how well-insulated you wish it to be. You may also be able to purchase these in pallets. It's made out of a glass-composites that are very lightweight and foamy. It's made from glass, which is spun into small fibres that are then woven to mats. These are either in rolls, or batts. Batts, which are large chunks insulation that fit into 2ft frames, have foil backings that reflect the heat and help prevent heat from escaping. This membrane keeps moisture out and stops small fiberglass particles entering the living room. The batts will be thicker to resist moisture, but they will shrink the interior space of the container.

It can cause skin irritation or breathing problems and is considered a hazardous building material. The symptoms include irritation of the skin, allergies, nose bleeding, asthma, rashes, and even serious infections. OSHA has posted a warning label for fiberglass. It is important to always use protective breathing and eye protection when handling or installing fiberglass. A humidifier that dampens air can prevent particles from being airborne. As warm water opens pores, it can push particles deeper into your skin.

Foam

In all insulation tests, spray foam beats fiberglass. Available in two main types:

open cell and closed cell foam. Spray foam is just as effective as fiberglass batts in creating an air-insulation barrier and it should be installed correctly. Spray foam has a minimum thickness requirement to be effective. It's not recommended to use spray foam in areas where there is extra insulation. You must also ensure there is no air in the container. Additionally, make sure that the foam does not pull away from the frame when it contracts in colder weather.

Closed-cell foams have a higher R, but they are more difficult to see once the entire cavity is filled. Also, you will need spot checks to ensure that the foam covers all of the framing. Open foam expands and fills the cavity. This makes it much easier to use. Closed cell insulation needs to have uniform thickness. Otherwise, heat will pass through the less insulated areas. A sign that your insulation isn't even is lat or lumpy insulation. Spray insulation should be placed in the right places. Colder steel will attract moisture and condensation, which can lead eventually to rust. It is possible to conduct a fog test using a simple fog machine to ensure that there are no leaks. If fog is seen coming from any part of the container, you will know that it is not air tight.

Spray foam installers must know the exterior of the building, including its shape and edges. They can spray inside conditioned and unconditioned areas and not just the interior. It is one of most expensive insulations so don't add it if it doesn't make sense. You can also spray insulation to the outside and beneath of your building, if you intend on making it look more traditional and covering it with a layer.

There are many different types of foam insulation. However, cellulose is the best. It is made from straws, sawdusts, cotton, hemp and other materials which are flame retardant. It's much more affordable than fiberglass and presents fewer health risks. Although it does not cause gassing as much as glass particles, you still need protection equipment and to breathe.

Panel Insulation

This type of insulation is the easiest to install and can be easily integrated into your framing. These presized panels are easy to fit in the gaps between the frames, much the same as blanket or fiberglass. Although they are thinner than other types of insulation, they cost more but have similar R ratings. The R rating for panel insulation is usually 7.5. Panel insulation outperforms fiberglass, and it has a thinner thickness which won't eat into your storage container. It is more expensive than spray insulation and cheaper.

Blanket Insulation

This insulation type is the most economical and is basically made of thin shredded fabric or rockwool. The insulation is applied in ready-made batts to the holes in the frame. It's thick enough to eat through your wall space, which is a challenge. You need to take safety precautions when blanket insulation is made of fiberglass. If you don't need cellulose foam, cotton and wool are eco-friendly choices. These natural choices can still get the R rating for construction standards. They are also more economical and less environmentally-friendly.

Living Roof

Living roofs can improve insulation. Although there won't be a section dedicated to roofing, it is an option design choice. A living roof is one that's made of plants and/or moss. It acts as a barrier between outside elements and the container. This is great for keeping the temperature in the container at a lower level in hot climates. However, it won't provide insulation in colder regions as the roof can allow heat to escape quicker.

Living roofs may be either flat or sloped. For shipping containers, a sloped layout is better because it encourages water drainage so there is no standing water that damages the steel. Living roofs are heavy and can reach 150kg/m2. This is why it is important to not install them if there have been any structural changes made to your container.

This is the layout of a typical living roof. It is recommended to use insulation for shipping containers because there is more possibility of heat and cooling escaping. In this instance, foam insulation is ideal externally as it creates water-tight barriers. Although plants need moisture, this is not what you need for your steel containers. The pond-liner provides an additional barrier that helps prevent moisture from reaching the container. The entire process of building a roof is explained in detail in this Instructable.

Chapter 6: Which Container Is Right?

Chapter 1 made it clear that you need to make many decisions when choosing which shipping container to buy. The next step is to determine whether or not you will actually purchase one. This chapter will provide information about the pros & cons of owning one, and floor plans on how to choose the layout.

A Container Home is a great investment.

1. It's eco-friendly: Many people end up building a container home for the "greener" aspect of it. Around the globe, thousands of steel containers are discarded. If you can save a landfill, that's even better.

2. Shipping containers are an economical alternative. You can easily

convert them into a house. Shipping containers can sometimes be purchased for free, making it much simpler to own one than a house with an attached price tag.

3. Construction Ease. You can assemble your home in just a couple days if you order all your shipping containers or containers to be pre-cut. This is definitely an advantage for the construction-illiterate homeowner.

Advantages of a Container Home

1. Insulation and Heat Control. Shipping containers are generally large rectangular steel sections. This is why shipping containers are more likely to absorb heat in the summer than cold in winter. You can overcome this issue with proper insulation. However insulation will take up less space within your home. A shipping container home

can be used to provide cooling in summer.

2. Rust is possible if you purchase a second-hand shipping container home. Shipping containers are quick to rust so if you decide to buy a shipping box that has been scratched or dented because you believe it gives your home more of a "manufactured", it's likely that it will eventually rust.

3. Potential Health Risques: It is important to remember that shipping containers were never intended as homes. It is possible that hazardous substances, such as lead and chromate, may be contained within the container's design. These toxins can lead to fatal consequences if exposed for long periods.

It is clear from the above that there are many arguments why you should or should not invest in a container-home. You as the consumer have the ability to choose the factors that matter to you. Spend time researching both good and bad.

Let's examine the pros & cons and then look at how you can design your container home based on floorplans or pictures from the past.

Keep it Simple

The simple layout of a twenty-foot home is shown in the first floor plan. As you can see the traditional doors which were used to get into the shipping container have been removed and replaced with a wall. This allows for the construction of a bathroom. The kitchen is the largest space of the house. However, there are barely any differences between the bathroom and the living area. In addition to being used as the living area, this floorplan also houses the bedroom. It is safe to say this container home of a particularly large size might be best suited for someone who lives alone.

A little bit more length

Although it is still a single bedroom, this floorplan is based on a larger forty-foot container. It is important to notice that the bathroom occupies the same space as in the previous floorplan. Due to the fact that the bathroom is typically the smallest area in the house, insulation will be more difficult in this area.

The original shipping container doors opening in that location makes the space surrounding it more drafty. In the previous floor plan, the bathroom area and the living area were the same in size. However, the forty foot plan offers both a bedroom area as well as a living space. The overall plan is more spacious.

Floorplans for Multiple Bedrooms

We will look at one floor plan with multiple bedroom units. This example has a storage unit measuring forty feet long. Two porches can be found in the house at separate locations. This allows two residents to enter the house through their own entrances. But, bedroom 1 is required to allow bedroom 2 to open to the kitchen, dining area, and living rooms. Another feature of this particular floorplan is that there are two skylights. One above the kitchen, and one in bathroom.

These floorplans can help you get a better understanding of the many ways that you can plan your container's layout. Let's take a look at some images of actual shipping container houses to get a clearer picture.

Even though the photo is not of an actual home, it still shows the stackable capabilities of a container house. Multi-story homes can be created by stacking three containers one on the other. The circular windows add an interesting twist to the space. Before you attempt to build this style of structure, check that you have the right zoning permits.

Explore all Possibilities

This last image is intended to demonstrate the potential of a shipping-container home. The bay window in the front of this home is an important feature. It gives the entire house a larger feel by making one part of it more visible to the natural light. This will help you when designing your container-house.

A budget-friendly way to purchase the Home of Your Dreams

The previous chapter may have made it feel like you want to move into a container-home immediately. But, it's not the right time to start talking business. This chapter will address the cost and options for a container-home, as well as how much you can afford. You will be able, depending on your budget and style to determine the price of various designer options. Also, the technical skills needed to build your own home instead of hiring a contractor.

Brass Tacks, The Cost of Materials

You can obtain a second-hand shipping container at no cost, as was stated previously. A used container will not be as accurate as a new one and could become less useful over time. Here's how much each step costs for your container construction. Shipping container homes are expensive because of how extravagant you like to travel and how large your finances.

Material

Cost breakdown

Container 20 Feet

The price range is between $1,400 and 2,800

40 Foot Container

Between $3.500 and 4.500

Flooring

Prices between $3,000 and $12,000

Glass Installation

Between $2,000 - $4,000

Heating and air conditioning

Between $3,000 and $7,000.

Plumbing

Between $3,000 and $7,000.

Electric

Between $3,000 and $7,000.

Roofing

Between $3,000 and $5,000.

Insulation

Between $4,500 and $5,500

Site Preparation - Housing Foundation

Between $8,000 - $14,000

These numbers will allow you to decide which route is the most cost-effective in terms both of construction and building materials. For $1,400 you buy a twenty-foot container. Next, add up each category. This would make your total approximately $36,000. The other aspect of your home to consider is whether you intend to hire a contractor who can help you with any special building skills.

A contractor's hourly cost starts at $50 and ends at $150. You can expect to pay more for your container home if you employ a contractor. A foundation is also an important part of the home that many people neglect. Although laying the foundation can have negative environmental consequences, it is also costly. If you don't have the skills to do this type of work, you can hire someone. Make sure you shop around for the best prices as you design and build your container home.

Going the prefabricated route

There is also the option to purchase a pre-fabricated shipping box home. The cost of these homes will range from $15,000 up to $215,000 but they can be very beneficial for you, especially if you don't have the necessary skills. There are three main companies who sell prefabricated shipping containers.

1. Logical Homes: Logical Homes designs your entire home for you. The company is a kind of architectural firm in that they take care of all the design, engineering and other tasks before you even receive your home. Below is a

photo simulation of Logical Homes building a container.

2. Meka - For a more Scandinavian vibe, visit Meka. This company's container houses look almost like they would be in an Ikea. Meka manufactures its products in the United States. This makes it easy to ship a container to your destination.

3. Nova Deko Modular Home Solutions - Based in Australia, this company provides a wide range container homes to fit all budgets. This one is currently available for $44,000.

A prefabricated shipping container home is a great option. However it can be more expensive than building it yourself. It is important to know what you need in a container home.

You should bring up whether or not foundation laying is included in your prefabricated home options when you talk with a company offering them. The foundation is a line item associated with building containers homes. This can be seen in the chart in this chapter.

What skills are required to build your house?

If you aren't sure if you want to buy your house pre-fabricated or build it from scratch, these are the skills you need in order to make a great shipping container.

1. Design skills: Before you nail the nails and hammer the nails, you have to plan how you will design your home. Google SketchUp is a fantastic tool that can assist you in this. Google SketchUp allows you to create and map a design.

The first step is to measure and sketch the plan.

2. Engineering skills: If you want to take out portions of the containers walls and put in new materials, then you must know how to properly reinforce the home. Even though minor cuts like inserting a window may not require much more than knowing how cut steel, bigger cuts might need some planning. You might use an angle grinder to make these cuts.

3. Knowledge of Welding: This includes knowing how to tackweld and, depending on your vision, arc welding. It is impossible to design windows, doors and other fixtures according to your aesthetic preferences without welding skills.

4. Concrete: To avoid any issues when you lay down your floor, ensure your subfloor is level.

It is safe to say this list does not include all the skills that you will need to create a container-home yourself. If you find yourself looking at the list and thinking you might not have the right skills, hire an architect, contractor, or engineer, or get a prefabricated container home. While it might be more costly, it will likely save you a few headaches.

Let's talk logistics: Transporting your shipping container

After you have bought your shipping box, it is time to figure out how it will be shipped to where you want to build. This step can be quite stressful, and many homeowners regret not having known about it before purchasing their shipping container. It is important to know where the container is being shipped from, how much insurance is required, as well as the costs of sitting the container. Although some of your choices in choosing the container may have an impact on how it will be transported, it is important to understand all your options.

The delivery cost and timeframe will depend on where your shipping container was shipped from. Most containers used will have been purchased locally and can be easily loaded on a truck to be delivered to your home. Delivery companies typically charge per mile. A standard twenty-foot container costs $2-6 per miles.

It is important to note that shipping costs can be affected by how big the container is. Shipping forty-foot containers is usually around 80-90% more expensive than shipping twenty-footers. It is important to know the type of truck being used to transport the containers. If you are able and able to unload the container using a crane/special forklift, a standard flatbed truck should suffice. A tilt bed truck is required if the container cannot be moved off the truck using a crane or special forklift.

If the foundation is easy to reach by the delivery truck, it will likely be possible for the truck to simply slide the container on top of its foundation. This is the easiest method for sitting. It is possible to rent a crane to lift the container off the truck, and then drop it onto its foundation. It is important to note that you can rent cranes and HIAB-loaders to load your container.

If the container is brand new, it was likely manufactured in Asia. The container will need shipping overseas. The two options are to have the container delivered empty and allow it to be transported to your destination as cargo. The first option ensures your container will arrive intact at your port. However you will need pay the full shipping charge, which can amount to several thousands of dollars.

A container can be used to transport freight, which is far more affordable. The freight company will pay delivery charges to have the goods shipped in the container. After that, you will take care of the delivery from your property to the port. This is also called a "one-trip", where the container is used to ship one item before being handed to another.

It is almost the same process as the local shipment. However, you are not expected handle the logistics of getting the container to port. You will need to communicate with freight companies to confirm when you expect your shipment to arrive. If you live near large international ports, you can be sure that your container will arrive on time as they are often delivered. Because it is less complicated than dealing through multiple companies, it is strongly recommended that you buy the container and arrange the delivery from one company. Shipped.com and J.B. Hunt provide convenient options for domestically shipped shipping containers.

If you purchase a container in another country, you will need to have Maersk Line handle the delivery. You can also move the containers yourself if your license is commercial. The cost of renting an automobile to do the job yourself is less than hiring a company. This is however not an option for many people. It all depends on whether the container will be delivered locally or internationally. The container can usually be delivered by local suppliers within a week to two weeks. But, the international route may take many months.

Insurance for containers is another option to add to your cost estimates and plans. Large freight companies often include insurance with their transportation costs. But some people consider it an upgrade. It is worth checking the actual value of your containers before purchasing insurance for delivery. Insurance is typically not necessary if there are only three or four containers left from your local supplier. However, many new containers sold overseas at several thousand per unit can be worth the extra investment. You can expect a lot on the 30-plus day journey from China, New York to China. It is always better to be prepared.

Location, location, location

Any new housing development brings forth several questions about zoning laws, building permits, tax codes, etc. Unfortunately, the country does not have a standard for shipping container homes. As we've discussed, a container home is a better option than a traditional residence. But, because it is a rapidly developing trend, regulators have yet to figure out how to handle it.

There is no standard for conducting inspections of these types of houses. Also, permit regulation is done at the county or municipality level. Therefore, there is no uniform approach. Before you begin building your shipping container home or any other type of construction, you must first do research in the locality where you plan to build.

A permit can only be issued if you have the necessary land. Before you begin to plan for this type of specialized housing, make sure to do your research. Certain areas may not be comfortable with this type building because of the unknown impact on property values. It is possible that remoter areas are more accommodating than cities and suburbs. Since it's easier for foundation construction and insulation to be installed, warmer climates with more firm soil (e.g. the southwest U.S.A.) are the best places to watch this trend. These areas have more experience with shipping containers and are more accepting of them. Draft all necessary plans for your project and present them to the local public work building department. To obtain a building permits in almost all cases, it is necessary to have scaled blueprints as well foundation plans and project specs. Next, talk to local authorities regarding the plans. Before you file your formal application, make any necessary changes to ensure that your building is up to code.

Before any physical construction begins, it is essential to get every permit you need and research all local planning laws. There are many horror stories about people who were forced to stop construction because they did not adhere to building regulations. Expect this tedious process to take at least a month. Permits can easily exceed $1000. Additional or modified work will require additional time and money.

The inspection is often the most difficult part of the building process. Any homeowner can attest. Routine inspections carried out by officials from the municipality form part of building regulation. This is done in order to make sure that everything is carried out according to the permit. During the construction of your container-home, you will need to schedule multiple inspections. The footing inspection is the first, which is normally done before the concrete foundation is laid. This allows you to verify that the soil is solid and the reinforcing poles are in place. After foundation construction is complete, the next inspection takes place. The remainder of your schedule may change depending on the regulations in your area. However, you may still need some as the project progresses. Most often after the insulation systems and ventilation systems are installed and then again once the basic utility structure has been completed.

After the project is finished, you will be able to have a final inspection. Sometimes, you will need to have multiple inspections on the same project. This can cause delays and make it difficult to move forward. Even though it can be exhausting, it is necessary. In order to not only comply with the law, but also to ensure your new home meets all security and safety standards.

It is important to know how to construct a foundation for your container-home. Concrete piers or slab-on–grade are two of the most common foundations that can be used to support shipping container homes. Concrete piers require only a concrete cube supported by steel bars. They are also the easiest to make. Two piers are laid for each corner of the container and one for the center.

This foundation provides extra ventilation and allows for more airflow since the container sits above the ground. Slab-on–grade (or a raft) is more common for soils with softer materials. This involves digging an excavation for concrete to be poured into. It is best to hire a qualified geotechnical or builder to ensure that the foundation and concrete type you choose are appropriate for your home's specifications.

Examples of concrete piers.

Normally, the container's actual weight is enough to keep it in place on its base. It is common to weld and bolt the containers directly into the foundation. Steel plates are placed at corners of the container to be able to support it before the concrete sets. Once the concrete has set, the containers can be welded onto the plates. You don't have to use welding if you do not want to. Simply drill through any fittings at the bottom and insert a 1 x 12-inch bolt. Shipping containers are strong enough for you to only fasten the corners. When connecting multiple containers together you will need to spray foam insulation at any connecting seams.

Chapter 7: How You Can Protect Your Home From The Elements

Now, you've moved the container onto your land and secured it into its foundation. It still needs to be habitable. Properly insulating it is perhaps the most important. Your house is designed to protect you from the outside elements. Without insulation, your home will be like a tin can. Your home's climate is a major factor in how it should be insulate. For cold and humid climates, insulation is more critical to ensure the house stays warm and prevent condensation. While ventilation and protection are not as important, they do require more. There are many kinds of insulation available, all with varying installation difficulty.

Spray foam has proven to the be one of most efficient insulating materials money can buy. It has an incredible R-value, which indicates the resistance to heat flow. Additionally, it prevents mold and corrosion by creating a continuous barrier of vapor. It is quick to install, can easily be applied to exterior and interior walls, and its consistency means that it can adhere to nearly all surfaces and fit into any gaps. The downsides to foam are its cost (estimated at about $850 per board feet, one shipping container would cost approximately $850 to insulate), and the mess. Aerosol foam requires protective gear, and it can be difficult to clean up after spraying.

Fiberglass insulation is the most widely used type. It is also more affordable than foam. This material comes in a blanket or rolled version and must be mounted on stud walls. This type can be used for almost all purposes. However you will need to install a vapor barrier in order to protect against condensation.

Insulation paneling can be another option. It is simple to install and offers a high R.value for its density. This product requires stud walls to be installed. Pre-fitted sections can be purchased to fit in between the studs. Paneling, which is slightly more costly than blanket fiberglass, is a good choice if you are looking to keep your insulation thin but still maintain a high value and don't have enough money for spray foam.

Spray foam insulation is applied on the inside and exterior walls of a container-home.

Fiberglass blanket insulation between wood studs.

Ventilation is essential for the preparation of your shipping container home. Ventilated homes are more likely to be kept cool during the summer and prevent condensation from causing mold and rust. The most common form of passive ventilation in containers is through simple vents. Vents, placed on the top and opposite sides of a container, provide airflow through the unit via the power of the winds.

Homes that are set on concrete piers (or other raised foundations) should include vents. They will help prevent condensation buildup and increase heat flow through your floors. This is especially effective in cold environments. These vents are also known as "whirlybirds" and are highly efficient in drawing out air from containers. These can be attached to the roof of your container in minutes and require only minor maintenance.

Example of a louvered exhaust and whirlybird generators attached onto a shipping container

In warmer climates, active ventilation may be needed to supplement passive systems to maintain the house cool. Many container homes employ extractor fans, which are exhaust-only systems, to draw out the warm air and humidity. These should be as high or higher than possible and away from the largest air source (typically a door, window).

Instead, supply-only ventilation systems actively push outside air into the unit. This is done by simply installing an air conditioning system on the side or container. A standard 12,000 BTU Heat/AC unit should be sufficient to cool a 40-foot container.

A container can be fitted with an exhaust-only extractor fan or a supply-only Heat/AC device.

Your shipping container home can be equipped with utilities just like any other house. Before you start building your home, make sure to draw up plans for the electrical as well as plumbing layouts. Before you start framing out the container's interior, be clear about where you want outlets and appliances to be. Consider the best location for the fusebox, and the hook-up to your power grid.

Before installing drywall on the walls, mark locations for the outlets and appliance plug-ups. You can drill holes through the studs to thread Romex wire through these holes, trying to be as efficient and as practical as possible. Many shipping containers come with holes at the base for easy access by a tractor. These holes can also be used to house parts of your circuit. Before insulation can be applied, the floors and walls should be cleared of any plumbing fixtures. The following illustrates an example of an electric plan.

Decorating Ideas for Shipping Container Homes

Shipping container homes can be thought of as quite unusual. However, interior design options might be equally as tricky for your home. This chapter will explain how you can decorate your home in a unique way that will enhance its overall design. Before you start looking for decor items to decorate your new and exciting home it's worth thinking about a larger theme. This will help you to feel more connected to the overall atmosphere of the entire space. This chapter will offer great tips and advice on how to save room, something every smart shipping container homeowner should try to do. Photos accompany every design recommendation to make them easier to comprehend.

Interior Design Option 1. Curtains

Many shipping container houses are dependent on curtains. Because of how dark a container dwelling would be without windows large and well-designed curtains are a necessity. Because of this, curtains are almost a necessity for shipping container homes. The following picture is an example of how curtains can maximize their use. The curtains are designed to cover both the porches and windows in the house simultaneously.

Interior Design Option 2, Reflective Glass

Although technically this is an exterior option, reflective glass can be used for your windows. The best part about reflective glass is that it allows you to see out from your windows even though others can't see in. Privacy is vital, even in remote areas. If your shipping container is near great views, reflective glass should be considered.

Interior Design Option 3. Stacking Rooms

A stacking of rooms or beds can be another way to optimize the limited space within your container home. You can see in the photo to the left that the sleeping space is below the living and TV viewing areas. Attached at the base of the living area is a rod covered with a thick dark curtains. This makes it possible to isolate the bed from the living and dining areas. You might find it difficult to sleep if there is someone watching television while you're getting ready for bed. But, when you live in a container house, the reality is that noise pollution could sometimes affect your space. You can also see in the photo how the decision was made not to place a bunk bed in the living area but to use the ceiling space. The lower bunk is equipped with a cushion to support it and can be used as an afternoon area or a bed to fall asleep.

Interior Design Option 4. Fold Out Table

A fold out dining table is an excellent way to design your kitchen in a container-home. This gives you greater versatility and usability. It allows for more square footage in the house, even when dinner is not being served. A foldable table can be folded out to provide more space for containers.

As you can see, the table is attached, as shown in the photograph below. This shelving unit could be used as both a bedroom and an eating area, according to the china in the dresser and books. This shelving unit also has openings on one end.

Pay attention to the drawers underneath your bed. A bench is found on top of each drawer and can be used to sit down while you eat. The drawer/bench combination can be used to seat up to four people.

Interior Design Option No 5: From Framed Photo to Table

The easiest way to fold a table is to leave its legs exposed on the walls. However, you can design or buy a collapsible folding table with a photo and/or painting on its bottom. As shown in the illustration, the legs can be used to frame the table when folded. This is a clever way to hide your table if it isn't in use. This idea is certain to attract comments when you invite someone into your home.

How to Add an Additional Room to Your Home

Step 1: Check Your Permits

Chapter 5 helped you understand the code and permits your shipping container must have in order to meet state regulations. If you are considering adding to your shipping container, make sure you review the codes and permits.

Step 2 Have a ready-made design

While it may seem redundant, I believe it's essential to have your added space mapped before you start construction. In some cases, shipping container homeowners believed they could add on to their home by simply drawing it on paper. Although the goal was for a larger home, the actual result was one of wasted time, money, or energy. Don't let this happen. You can design your addition and then hire outside help if needed.

Step 3 Choose the Area in Your House That is the Most Used

Let's imagine that you already own a forty-foot shipping box home and that you want to expand it. Let's say that you are expecting a little one and know that your current home is not large enough to accommodate them. When creating the plans for an addition to your home, it is important to consider the best location and minimize disruption to your existing home details. For example, you might believe that the bathroom would make the best location to add a bathroom and remodel it, but this is unlikely. Take into consideration your plumbing expenses. If you decide to knock out the bathroom, and then rebuild it in a new area of the house you will need to pay another person for the plumbing fixtures. This is why it's important to choose an area of the home that isn't being used.

These same principles apply to shipping container homes. Sometimes it can be acceptable for them to take on an odd shape after they are built. You can remove the large wall in your living space and attach an extra shipping container. When designing your addition, be creative and make changes as minimal as possible.

Step 4 Set clear priorities

Find a way that you can keep the huge bay window in your house if it's an area you love. You don't have to compromise on the window's location, even though it would be the most convenient. You have to figure out a way that it can all be included in your overall plan. If you cannot keep it all, you will discover this in time. You can then alter your plans.

Step 5: Consider Connecting Containers via Doorway

The foundation of your container home will need to be laid. A contractor may be needed to help you. But, the design of your shipping containers' connections isn't difficult. You don't have to cut the steel of your existing unit to match the larger opening of the new shipping containers. Instead, use a small door cutting to connect the two units.

You won't need a lot of holes in your shipping container units if your design is simple. This will allow you to only cut a hole about the size of your doorway. This will save your time as well as reducing the need to hire someone to do this job.

How to be Handyman and Provide Maintenance for Your Container

A shipping container home can be built or purchased for less than a mortgage that you will have to pay for the remainder of your life. However, this is still a very small fraction of the cost. A shipping container home should be treated as an investment. This chapter will explain how to extend the life span of your shipping container. A shipping container, or any other type of home, that is new to the market, should not be purchased only for it to fail due to environmental pressures. This chapter will show you how to be a responsible homeowner and reduce the wear-and-tear on your home. These techniques will increase your home's value over the long term.

Tactic I: External Cladding

External cladding can be considered the equivalent of a protective coating or skin. This will protect your home against weather and other factors that can damage it over time. Cladding does more than protect the steel exterior of the shipping box home. External cladding is also a great way to improve the appearance of the steel quality and make it look more modern. To weatherproof or improve the appearance of your home's exterior, there are several types of cladding available:

* Stone cladding
* Timber cladding
* Weatherboard cladding
* Brick cladding
* Fiber Cement cladding

External cladding can be added to your home to prevent termites or rot. External cladding is durable and can last up to 50 years. Cladding is available for as low at $3.00 per square or as high as

$40.00 per square. The wide price range can offer many options.

Tactic #2: Treat Rust Areas Faster

We've spoken briefly about the dangers of rust on shipping containers. You can avoid expensive decisions by treating areas quickly. Although you can remove rust with home ingredients such as lemons, it is not recommended to use on valuable items like your container house. If you want maximum results against any rust that has built up, then try the following combinations of products:

* 7 cups lime-free vegetable glycerin

* 1 cup sodium citrate. This product can also be purchased at your local drugstore

* 6 cups of lukewarm tap water

* Powdered calcium Carbonate (also known under the name chalk).

Keep adding more chalk until you get a paste. Spread your paste mixture over the rusty area with a spreader or other tool. Allow it to set up until it becomes hardened. Once your paste is dry, you can scrape off any remaining residue using a metal tool such a chisel and prong. This should eliminate any rust. However, it's possible to get it back by using a chisel or prong. Container homeowners should look out for rust frequently, as it is a common problem on these homes.

Aside from the fact that you will receive the shipping container, it is likely that there will be damage to your roof due to how they are typically shipped. If you are building your first home, be sure to remove the dents from your roof. This will save your time in the future.

Tactic 3 is to use Corrosion Resistant Paint

Applying corrosion-resistant spray paint to your container home can be another way to maintain it. To prevent future corrosion, this paint can be applied to your home as soon as it is built. This paint can be applied to an area that has already rust but it is more of an attempt at fixing the problem than a preventative measure. Use corrosion resistant paint at the beginning of your home to avoid any potential eye irritations caused by rust.

Tactic 4, Grease

A different way to prevent rusting or sticking is to apply grease. These areas include door hinges from the shipping box unit (if you wish to keep them), window jams, door handles, and door handles.

Shipping containers are very durable and last for decades. They can also be transported internationally and abroad. However, many people haven't used them as their homes for a long time so it's difficult to see how much they can last or what their greatest limitations might be. The main limitation in maintenance seems to be rust. It should be avoided that rust accumulates. If rust does happen, the solvent in this chapter is sure to help eliminate it. As with all types of injuries, if you can avoid a significant problem by taking small and frequent measures, this is the best option to avoid major problems down the road.

Chapter 8: Types, Shipping Container Homes

Many building designs can be made from shipping containers. These containers can be used to make functional buildings. It's also very cost-efficient. However, not everyone is comfortable with the idea of shipping containers as a building material. When designed properly, shipping containers can easily be distinguished from traditional homes. This section will explain the different shipping container home types that you are able to build.

Off-Grid Cabin

Shipping containers make an excellent base to build an offgrid cabin. The best part about building an offgrid cabin out of a shipping container, is that it can be expanded and modified in any way you like. You don't have to make any additions to your on-grid cabin. You can simply use the rectangular design of the container to create the structure of your offgrid log cabin. You can build your off-grid cabin in a short time. The downside is that you'll have to make the most of your space to make your home more useful.

Ranch Style Home

A standard 40' shipping box has 67.5m3 total area, while a 20' one is 33.1m3. You can construct a lavish ranch-style home by stacking 6 shipping containers. A standard 40' shipping container has a total area of 67.5m3, while a 20' container is 33.1m3. You can also make a two-storey ranch house by using the shipping container structure above it as the floor.

Emergency Shelters

Containers can be used as emergency shelters in order to provide temporary shelter to people during times of crisis, such a natural disaster or domestic violence. Shipping container shelters provide better protection than tents or other temporary shelters. Furthermore, they can last for a longer time and are more resistant to harsh weather conditions. Shipping containers are affordable and can be used by organizations to provide shelter for their clients. Shipping containers are also designed to be sustainable in order to meet the needs of the global environment crisis. Many countries worldwide use shipping containers as emergency shelters for people who have been affected by natural disasters or wars.

Construction Trailers

Many shipping container homes are used as construction housings. Sometimes construction projects require workers to stay on the site. Therefore, building from shipping containers is an efficient way to save time and money. Additionally, construction trailers built from shipping containers are mobile so they can be removed from the site immediately after construction is completed.

Campers

If you're a serious DIY enthusiast, you can convert a 20' container vehicle into an RV-camper. Because shipping containers come in a shape that is easily pulled by suitable flatbeds they make RV campers a great choice. An RV camper constructed from shipping containers can still be equipped with the same features as conventional RVs. It's cheaper to purchase an RV camper built from shipping containers than a brand-new RV.

School Buildings

Many organisations around the globe now use shipping containers to create school buildings that can be durable and safe for children. It is trendy to build school from shipping containers. They can be used to construct youth centers and other educational facilities, where children can receive instruction in academic subjects. It is possible to make many types of buildings from recycled shipping boxes.

Shipping containers are ideal for all types of homes due to their versatility. They are also ideal for building the bases of buildings because their rectangular shape allows for flexibility and provides support for future expansions.

Planning and Building Process

Planning phase is the most important aspect of any project. The same applies to a shipping container house. Modern and new homes tend to not follow the budget. Most modern homes go over budget by 20%. It is essential to establish a solid plan to follow it. This holds true even for shipping containers.

These are some of the things you should consider when you're planning to build a shipping box home.

Set the Budget

The first step is to decide the cost of your shipping container home. If you only have $20,000. You don't need to plan a house over 4,000 square feet. It doesn't make sense to plan a house that spans over 4,000 square feet if you only have $20,000. You must keep at least 20% for contingencies. This is your "reserve money" and you can use it as a reserve to pay for any unexpected expenses that you may face during the construction. Most times, unexpected expenses will occur when you build a shipping containers home.

Let's consider an example for how to calculate the contingency. Let's take $150,000 as your budget. You need to reserve 20% of the budgeted money as a reserve. This would translate into a reserve fund amount of $30,000. Take $30,000 off the total budget. You can then use this amount for construction. Do not base your design on $120,000.

2. Decide on the Design, and then finalize it

You now have the budget in place to build your home. Now it's time to begin designing. Setting a realistic budget is essential to ensure that your home design doesn't go overboard. You can build a home from a single container or an entire mansion depending on your needs and budget. Shipping containers can be combined in many different ways so you can create the perfect home with everything you need. Your best approach to designing and planning your house is to focus on the most useful aspects first before you get into details.

You need to determine:

* How many canisters do you require?

* How many persons will live with you in your home?

* Do you have to worry about how to insulate your container home?

* What will the home be used for?

Slowly go through each step, and then decide what is most important. As you make progress, you can add to the plan. For you to build the perfect house, your answers must be clear. If you decide to change your mind, you'll end up spending more. Don't try to tear down the wall of the container only to put it back together again. This will only increase you budget. It is not necessary to plan your house carefully in order to avoid extra costs.

Determine Who Builds Your Home

Once you have established the design and chosen the person to build the shipping container house, you need to decide who that person is. Many people choose to build shipping container homes from scratch. This is more rewarding than buying a home. Learn the skills needed to build a house. If you lack experience and time, it is worth looking into hiring the right person for the job. Hiring a contractor is the best choice, as they are more experienced. A contractor can construct your house in a very short time. But hiring a contractor will make the job more expensive. Before you hire the contractor, take the following into consideration:

* Ask people to provide references

* Ask the contractor if they offer a guarantee

* Learn the specifics of the insurance contract, if they have insurance for liability.

Shipping Container Location

Now you have created the budget, determined the number and design of the home, as well as the person responsible for building it. Now you need to decide where to build your house. You must design your house according to your personal preferences and where your family will live. Be sure to determine your preferred location before you start working on the design.

The first step is to find the right area to build the shipping container. You can search the internet for land or use Zillow to find out where the shipping container will be moved. It's also worth speaking to the locals as they might know of any areas that are available.

After you have determined the correct piece of land for your home, contact the local planning & zoning department. You should speak with them to understand their decision and whether they will grant permission to you to build your own home. If the local municipality refuses to give you permission, then you may need another piece.

Determine if the Home is Possible

Determine if you have enough resources and the skills to build a shipping-container house. It requires a lot more work, time and money. To construct a shipping container, you will need to have money and time.

These are the essential resources you need. You must also know how to do this yourself. You can transform the container into a house by hiring an architect or someone who will help you change the inside. Also, consider whether or not you intend to purchase building material before you start construction. A container cannot be purchased and used to build a home in a remote area, such as a yard or port 2,000 miles away. You will have to spend a lot of money and take some time getting the container to you.

Also, consider the permits and building planning. You will need permissions from both the state or the community in which you live. This is a very sad truth. In most places around the world, it's not possible to obtain a building license quickly. It can take you time to obtain permits if the state does have no regular laws and has no planning department. If you find yourself in this situation, it is worth considering moving to another state or city with different zoning regulations and planning laws.

Find the best way to ship a container

Once you've made the decision to build your shipping container home, you must ask yourself what type of approach you will use.

There are a few options that you can use to build a house. After laying the foundation, you can begin to build your house. Once your house is completed, you can't do much except extend it, knock it down, or start all over again.

Shipping containers offer a number of different options.

Built on-Site

The house can be built directly on the ground or moved when it is ready. This works best if your land is accessible and you don't have to worry about getting tools. It allows you to build your house for as long and as many hours as you like. Also, you can minimize the amount of moving that you need by planning ahead.

When you purchase a shipping box, you'll need to first have it delivered to a place and then move it to the spot where you plan to build the house. Directly to the building site will reduce the moving process and make it easier when you finally move it in.

If you have the ability to use equipment, and you prefer a simpler build, then it might be a good option. It is possible that your land does not contain any resources, so you will require power and other utilities in order to build.

Building off-Site

Many cities and towns will have offsite workshops that you can use to rent space for building and working on projects such as shipping containers. While the exact facilities you have available will vary, they will all allow you to begin building the area indoors and provide you with a lot more tools and equipment.

This will ensure that your things are safe and easy to find. Once the exterior is completed, it's time to move the container and install the plumbing and wiring.

If you want to build the container by yourself, it may be more difficult and costly than building on-site. You need to get out of work during working hours. Your team will also need you.

You'll need a permit to use their facilities. Many places are more than willing to do the work but don't want uninsured cowboys stealing their space.

It depends on how you set up your building. All things considered, the cost for transporting the container, renting the space, and using the tools might be comparable. If you work on-site, you have the right to access the tools and can work for as long or as you like. There is also no risk of a heavy unit being moved and transported.

Prefabricated Homes

Third, the shipping container can be prefabricated and placed on site by other people.

This option lets you have basic shipping containers converted to ready-to use, but you will still need to give input. The containers can be built to your specifications or can be made to pre-made designs and placed in place. This option can be quite expensive, with several designer containers going for as high as $200,000.

You may save your time and energy. If you don't have the skills, this might be cheaper than hiring someone to do the job. Your time is worth something. Planning and saving a few hundred hour might mean you're making more money.

If you're interested in playing a key role in building the house then you should ask yourself what you really value. Is it your intention to simply renovate a property? Do you desire a house that matches your requirements? Do you need a complex project?

If you really want to build a home for the long term, then you will need help. The real question is, how much do YOU want to do this yourself?

Checklist for Building Process/Checklist

Although each container house will be unique, the basic steps of construction are consistent. The right order will help you avoid costly setbacks. This will help you get your project done faster by following these steps.

1. Make your interior and exterior designs for your new home. Your blueprint for each stage of your project is the design you have come up with.

2. Consult a contractor as well as an engineer when building a container house. Even if your contractor won't be hired, their expertise will help you avoid unexpected complications.

3. Create your design to help you decide the type of container that will best suit your new home.

4. Lay the foundation to your house. While you wait to receive your containers, make sure to prepare your foundation in advance so it can go into place immediately. While some

containers can be delivered in as little as a few days, others may take up to four months. If you want your container to arrive on time, make sure that you have everything ready. It will keep you from moving the container again once it is poured.

5. Place the containers in the foundation. A crane is required to place the containers on the foundation. This crane will likely be rented. A crane can be used to make sure the container gets on the right foundation. There are many options, but cranes make it the fastest and easiest way to place your container.

6. Connect the containers. If you are planning to use multiple containers, this is the right time to connect them. It is best to have some welding experience. However, it might be faster to hire a professional to work with clamps, bolts or other materials to fix the containers.

7. Reinforce your structure. Reinforce the container.

8. Add your roofing. Sometimes, a roof might not be required. If the container's roof looks good, it is probably not necessary. It is time to construct a roof if you absolutely need one.

9. Take out all of your openings. Next, cut out the openings of the windows and doors in your home. There are some home designs that require the removal of an entire side wall. If this is not your experience, hiring a contractor will save you time and money.

10. Now, add the flooring. Once the roof is in place, you can move on to the flooring. Containers are notorious for causing a lot damage to the flooring. If the container floor is in good order, you can simply coat it with epoxy coating or polyurethane. You may find floors that are in very poor condition in some containers. In this instance, it may be

necessary for you to completely replace the floor.

11. Sealing. Sealant is needed to fill in any spaces created by cutting or removing walls. This could involve welding in certain areas. Other areas might require caulking, spray foam, and rods.

12. Weatherproofing. This is in addition to sealing your home. You must seal any cracks or openings in your home to keep out the elements.

13. Install doors and Windows

14. It is important to frame your interior. Frame the interior.

15. Install the subfloor. The subfloor is optional, but it is something that many container homeowners prefer to do. It serves as an additional barrier between home's actual structure, and any residues left over from the materials used. It is as simple as laying concrete

flooring on top of the container's original floor.

16. Install the plumbing system and electrical wiring.

17. Insulation can be added to protect you from the extreme temperatures outside. There are extreme temperatures in certain places, so the steel container construction can make it impossible to live there. Insulation allows you to maintain control over the temperature of your home.

18. While your container home should be complete and ready to go, there are still some finishing touches. It is time to install appliances and fixtures and make your new container home liveable. It is time to landscape your area so that it blends in with its natural surroundings.

Home Plans

Here are several samples plans that offer many design options. These are just some examples. These should give an idea of how to organize your shipping containers into a home that is beautiful.

Plan 1

209,7 sq. feet

- 2 beds

2 person space

2 Container Blocks for 20 ft. and 10 ft.

The first sample plan includes two containers blocks each of 20 ft.x9ft. This one is enough space for two. It boasts 209.7 sq. ft. It includes a combination living and kitchen area as well as a bedroom.

Plan 2

- 320.3 square feet
- different planning options
Large kitchen and living room
- big bedroom
- Space for 3
- 1 container block for 40 ft

Plan 2 is a wonderful example of a 40-foot container dwelling. The design includes a living room, kitchen, bedroom and bathroom. This simple design can easily accommodate three people on 320.3 sq. There are two design options. The decision is up to you.

Plan 3

- 304,5 acres
- 1 bedroom
Large kitchen and living room
- Space for 2-3 persons
- Terrace
- 2 container blocks for 20 ft

Plan 3 illustrates a two-to-20 foot container home. The simple design of the home is minimalistic. It measures 304.5 sq. This home can comfortably host two to three people. It includes a bedroom and a large area for the living room and kitchen. The room is large enough to fit a dining area so everyone can comfortably eat together. The terrace offers privacy and fresh outdoor air.

Plan 4

385,57 square foot

- 2 bedrooms

Large kitchen and living room

- For 3-4 persons

- Terrace

2 container blocks for 20 feet and 1 containerblock for 10 feet

The next sample plan consists of two 20 ft. and one 10 ft. Container blocks. It's designed to provide enough space for a patio. This design can comfortably accommodate 3-4 persons within 385.57 Sq. ft. It offers two bedrooms and one spacious bath, along with a large and open kitchen and living space.

Plan 5

- 470 feet

Two bedrooms

Large living and dining room with large kitchen

- 4 person space

- Terrace

2 container blocks per 40 ft, 20 ft

Plan 5 gives you a T shape-like design. It consists two container blocks of 40 ft.x9ft. and 20 by9ft. It measures 470 square feet. It's a great space for 4 people. You will see it has a large kitchen and living room, a bathroom that is accessible to all and two bedrooms. (One master bedroom has its very own bathroom). You can add outdoor furniture to your terrace or deck, making it the ideal setting for a spring and fall evening. It is perfect for any type of gatherings you may want in your shipping container.

Plan 6

619.1 square feet

Large living space

- separate kitchen

2 bedrooms are available for children

- 1 big master bedroom

- Room for 4

3 container blocks per 20 ft. 2 container blocks per 10 ft.

This home plan was built using 5 shipping containers. It boasts 619. This is the perfect size for a small family of four. It is spacious enough that you can make it your home.

Plan 7

- 380 feet

2 levels

- 1 big master bedroom

Space for 3

2 container blocks for 20 feet and 1 containerblock for 10 feet

The stunning 483 square feet of space can be created from two 20 foot-long container blocks and one 10 foot-long container block. The floor area is 483 sq. This design is ideal as it can comfortably accommodate 3 people. The upper floor features a master bedroom with en suite bathroom. The lower floor hosts a large living room, a cozy kitchen, and secluded bathroom. The design is elegant and simple, giving the house an elegant facade.

Plan 8

- 550.8 square feet
- 2 levels
Large kitchen and living room
- 1 big master bedroom
Space for 5

- Terrace

1 container block per 40 ft, 2 containers blocks for 20ft and 3 containers blocks for 10ft

This plan uses three shipping container sizes (40 ft. x 20 ft. x 10 ft. It has a large 550.8 sq. It boasts a large 550.8 sq. One bedroom is on the upper level and has direct access to a balcony. It also features an efficient combined dining room/kitchen, and a living space that provides ample space to entertain visitors.

Plan 9

613 square foot

- 2 levels

Large kitchen and living area

- separate kitchen

- 2 big master bedrooms

Space for 5

- 2 terraces

3 container blocks per 20 ft. 2 container blocks per 10 ft.

You can see that this architectural plan has five containers and covers a large area of 613sq. The floor area is 613 sq.ft. It also has two floors. This design is usually more expensive than the average shipping container house. The good news is that it's a cost-effective option for those with the means to make their home bigger than traditional homes. This spacious design was created to meet the needs of all family members. Separate terraces are available for small gatherings and to let you enjoy some fresh air.

Plan 10

942 square foot

- 2 levels

Large kitchen and living room

- 2 big master bedroom

- Room for 5

- Terraces

1 container block is 40 ft long, 3 containerblocks are 20 ft each and 2 containers blocks are 10 ft.

The final design includes six shipping containers that form a large shipping container home. It totals 942 sq. The home can accommodate a family with five in size and has 942 sq.ft. It includes 2 big master bedrooms, 2 bathrooms, large kitchen, and living room. You can also have a balcony, thanks to the two-story structure.

These are just a few ideas of plans you might want. You have the choice to ignore them all, or go into detail with each one. You can also copy the contents of each plan and create your design with what you have in your mind and what you can afford. You don't have to limit your creativity. The choice of room type and location is entirely up to the individual.

Chapter 9: Site Preparations

You must make preparations for your container before it is delivered. If you do not plan your stage properly, it is likely that you will end up paying more than originally planned. These steps will ensure that your site is prepared for receiving the container. Let us help you by highlighting some important things that you should consider.

Pick the right location

First, determine where you want to place your container. It is which part of your land grid do you need it to be? What factors will influence your decision? These are just a few of the questions we'll be answering.

Sun and Shade

Sunlight is another important aspect to be aware of. Even though it can be quite pleasant to let the sun bathe your skin on a cold winter morning, the sun can also make you feel hot. Be sure to observe your surroundings and choose places that are bright enough to allow sunlight in. If you plan to put your container in a sunny place, you may want an air conditioner.

The best way to help your container is to place it under a shaded spot or under a few trees. However, you will need to remember that trees often shed their leaves in winter and fall. Sun Calc, a program that calculates the height of sun at any point in the world, can help you make these calculations. It can work at any time. You can also use it to calculate the height of the sun for any given day.

Topography and Drainage

This is due to your land's shape and slope. This is how water will run off the land when it rains. You wouldn't want to see water puddles, or sticky mud in your container. It could cause a lot of damage. This will allow you to adjust the flow of water across the area.

Water can unfortunately be a habitat for snakes or mosquitoes.

Views

This section is where your thoughts turn to what you see through the doors and windows of your container. Sometimes, a view over a hill, valley, moving water body, or another object can enhance the beauty and appeal of your container. Place your container so you can have a good view of all around you.

Access

Imagine how you will get into the container via major roads. What length should the path be? What angle of elevation should it be? Should steeps be included or should they be excluded? Are you able to remove any obstructions from the path? What about trees or other vegetation? Do you see the views change as you travel up the road. You will also need to create a walkway that can be used by trailers or building contractors. It must be sufficiently wide and well-equipped with angles and turns to ensure the best work output.

Preparation for Ground Inspection

You must ensure that the ground is stable enough to hold the containers and large amounts of furniture. You must consider not only the terrain but also the foundation to hold the containers in their place. A variety of foundations can be used, including beams (piers), trench foundations, piles and trench foundations. The type of soil used on the job site will affect the choice you make.

There are many types and styles of soil. Each one needs a unique approach. Before you can test the soil, make sure it is able to bear large amounts of weight over time without crumbling. You should have the soil tested to determine if it's a sandy soil or a mixture.

It's possible the rock or gravel could be used. The soil's response to stress is different so it is important to consider the type and weight of the foundation.

These are the most frequent soil types that can be used to build a container home.

Soil With A Lot Of Sand

* It is made primarily from tiny particles. However, it also contains some gravel and rock.

* One of the hardest soil types. It is able to withstand loads well, provided that the load is not concentrated in a single spot.

* Experts recommend that foundations not be buried too deep in order to avoid damaging the soil.

* This soil can be used with the beam foundation, which is a popular

foundation that can easily be constructed quickly.

Clayey

Clay soil retains more water than sandy soil and can be more difficult for builders to work with. It is risky to work with wet soil, as it can sink and become unstable.

Clay work can be very expensive. The site must be prepared for future loads.

* Most likely you will need to dig soil more stable that clay, then pile foundations or trenches are used to support the structure.

Rocky

* Advantage - Very strong and can bear a lot of weight

* Negative: It is difficult for people to work with.

The best way to begin is to make sure the ground is level and clear of any irregularities that could compromise the foundation's holding power. Experts recommend supporting loads as much as possible. Concrete piles in this instance are the best option. You can drill through the rock until you reach the required depth. Once that is done, you can begin to lay the concrete foundation.

Gravel

* Advantage: Gravel can be used for drainage.

* Disadvantages: Gravel is not as strong as rocks, so you need to build foundations.

First, you need to dig the gravel to the required depth. After that, the surface needs to be levelled and the foundation needed to support it. The trench foundation is for gravel soils.

How to identify which type of soil is present in your region

You cannot tell which kind of soil it is by simply looking at them. One type of soil might appear at the top, but we could be looking deeper to find another. It is important that you get it right from beginning.

1. Use the expertise of a geotechnical specialist to help you identify and describe the soil type you are dealing with.

2. He will also tell you the best foundation to build for the soil.

3. The ground will be drilled every 100 feet to 150 feet by the geotechnical expert. These holes will inform the engineer about the soil type and, therefore, its bearing capacity.

Site Works

This will include all the processes that you will need in order to prepare your construction site for your container's installation. In order to avoid ruining any one of these things, you might be required to follow a certain sequence.

Let's now discuss some activities that occur here.

Staking and Marking

This is the best thing that you can do.

1. Mark the ends in which your container will go.

2. Mark the sites where utilities, roads, etc., will be built.

3. Marking can be done with paint, or wooden sticks attached to ropes.

Clearing and Grubbing

1. If you see any, remove it.

2. Reduce the number of trees, stumps, and rocks.

3. The more vegetation on the land, you will need to clear it more often.

Grading and cutting, as well as filling

1. The foundation of your container can be chosen here. You can choose to grade the flooring uniformly or stick with the uneven.

2. Concrete or raised slabs are possible to grade the ground.

3. Make sure to add berms (swales) to protect your container home against flood waters.

4. Fix culverts or bridges to water flow points.

Road building

1. Use concrete or asphalt to fill the roads leading you to your container.

2. Avoid using heavy equipment to avoid roads being damaged.

Controlling Erosion

1. The land is most susceptible to erosion if it has been cleared of all vegetation and dirt.

2. Sometimes, erosion is caused either by rain or the accumulation and disintegration of sediments from ponds and streams.

3. You can prevent erosion by planting beneficial vegetation around the area where your container will be sat.

4. You might also consider using erosion control equipment such silt barriers and wattles.

5. For more information about water pollution or erosion, please contact your state's Environmental Quality Office.

Foundation

You should consider the type and foundation of your container's foundation when you are building it.

Is foundation required for containers?

The foundation is important for your container. Ground often undergoes shifting and sliding, thereby affecting your container's level. A foundation will provide a solid leveling. Even more so if you're working with many containers. It is possible for your containers to be separated by shifting in the ground.

There are other materials that could affect the level of your floor, such as clay or rocks. A more level foundation will make your container weigh less and spread evenly on the ground. Your container's foundation would also be free from rust and moisture problems.

Which Foundation Is Best?

There are four main types you can use to build foundations for your container. These are the most common foundations, so you may want to decide which one is best for your needs.

Pier Foundation

* They are the most used foundations to build container homes.

* It's easy to construct and can be done alone.

* It can be done quickly.

* This foundation is built with concrete blocks. Each block has a dimension of 50cmx50cmx50cm.

* Concrete reinforced with steel can increase its strength.

* They are generally placed at the corners.

* Four are required for twenty-foot containers. Two additional will be needed to support the center of the forty-foot containers.

* As you won't need to dig up any earth, you save both time and money.

* The only digging that you should do is for the piers.

* You don't need any special or technical tools or know-how in order to construct this type of foundation.

Pile Foundation

* This foundation is most effective for soils with poor drainage.

* You push piles into the weak soil until you reach a point where the soil is more stable and rigid.

Once you place the piles in solid ground, pour a lot more concrete to keep them there.

* This is not something anyone can do. This could mean that you need technical expertise and support.

* A pile driver, which is an example of the tool required for this foundation, can be used.

Slab Foundation

* This foundation can also take place on soils that have low carrying capacity.

* It takes time for one to be erected.

* You will need plenty of soil.

* You will need a concrete slab in order to support your containers.

* Use an 18-feet slab by a 42feet length for a 40feet container. This dimension can be used to provide additional foundation in the area not occupied by your container.

* It gives your container rigidity, stability, and strength.

* You don't have termite issues to worry about.

* They are more expensive and harder to erect.

* They're built in warm regions, since the slabs help to transfer heat from the container into the ground below.

* However you may not be in a position to see any connections beneath the slab foundation. Most likely, you will have to dismantle the slab.

Strip Foundation

* Also known as trench foundation.

* It is a mixture of the ideas used to create the slab and piling foundations.

* The concrete strip used for support is here.

* The concrete strip is approximately two feet across and four feet deep.

* You can choose to make strips for the containers' outer edges, or at their top and bottom.

* It's cheaper than the slab foundation, but not as stable.

* If the ground is normally wet and loose, you can run a rubble section below the foundation.

* This foundation is resistant for earthquakes.

* They are the best foundation to support small and medium-sized containers.

Concrete Quality For Foundation

The first thing that comes to mind when someone decides to buy a concrete box is its strength. The concrete strength that you will need for your house is determined by geotechnical professionals. C rating stands for concrete strength. Concrete C15 is the most well-known all-purpose concrete. It contains five parts cement, five portions gravel and two pieces of sand. Concrete will become stronger if it is made up of more cement. C30 is an example. It contains three times as much cement, gravel and sand than the average concrete. You can use your hands to mix small amounts. You can also choose a cement mixer.

You must make sure the concrete is properly mixed, even if you mix it yourself. Failure to do so will result in a significant decrease in concrete strength. You only need to count how many cubic meters your foundation is in order calculate the concrete required. Multiply 22 x 10x2 to determine the concrete needed for a baseplate that is 22 feet long and 10 feet deep. The required concrete quantity is 440 cubic inches.

Concrete is not recommended to be placed in very hot conditions. To block direct sunlight, you can put temporary shades. The concrete must be sprayed with cold water before being poured. For optimum temperatures, pour concrete in the morning and late at night.

Transporting, Receiving, and Preparing Containers

Transport of containers

Once you have purchased your shipping containers, you will need to have them shipped to your place. You should also consider the type of transport you prefer, as you did in the previous steps. Remember to keep your transportation costs under budget. It is better to have your container shipped for less than you budget. This would be another way to save some money.

Cooperating with the Dealer

Try to negotiate a price with the dealer that sold the container. This will help reduce your transportation costs. You should remember to factor in the cost for transporting the container if this is something you wish to pursue.

If the dealer is within walking distance of your location, you can easily opt for this option. A crane can be used for lifting the container off the truck. Renting a crane is required, but it's not necessary if your dealer will be transporting your container. Most dealers will use a swingthru truck that includes a crane that assists in lifting the container.

Transport the container by yourself

While it's not expensive for the dealer to deliver your container, there are many benefits to building your own shipping container home. Because you're building your container home, why not ship the container yourself?

To do this, you'll need to rent truck and crane. Commercial drivers licenses are required in order to rent a truck. A CDL can make it easy to rent a truck, especially if you take ease-of-access into consideration when you secure the site. Maybe a family member, friend or acquaintance has a CDL. You can either pay them something or get them to drive your truck.

This option tends be less expensive than having your container shipped by the dealer, unless your dealer is willing to negotiate a lower shipping cost. This isn't necessarily the most affordable option.

Rent a Lift bed

A truck with a liftbed attached to it is the best and cheapest way to transport your container. The rental cost of either a crane, or forklift is not necessary. Depending upon whether you have a CDL or not, you have the option of either driving the truck yourself or having it done by someone else.

This method of offloading and delivery is simple. The truck is moved to the foundation and backed up. The foundation is lifted and the container slid onto it. The crowbar can push the corners to make small adjustments to container positioning.

Receiving the containers

It is a very exciting day for many shipping container home builders. All the research, preparation and work you put into this project is finally starting to show results. Your shipping containers will be delivered on a day full of tasks. You want them all to go smoothly. This section will address some of what you need to know in order to get your shipping containers delivered.

Container Anchorage

An anchor should be used to secure a shipping container. This is for safety reasons so that it doesn't tip over due to unforeseeable weather events. Anchors also reduce the possibility of damage from shaking.

There are many options to anchor your container. The choice of method will depend on several factors, starting with the type and quality of the foundation.

1. Welding - This is an excellent method to anchor your container. For anchoring the container, you must attach steel plates while pouring concrete.

Once containers are permanently attached to the foundation, they can't be altered.

Keep in mind, however, that it may be very difficult for you to move the container house, or make other changes to the overall structure.

2. Bolting: Through holes can be made in the container floors. Once they are attached to their foundation, bolt them in place. Drilling usually takes place at the corners. Bolts that are 12 inches in length and 12 inch wide can then be added. If needed, bolts can be used as a way to join multiple containers.

Clean the Container

You should have all your containers fixed to the foundation, and the cases connected to one another. It is important to clean your containers' interiors, even though there is still much to do. Your containers might have been transporting hazardous chemicals. It is important to clean them thoroughly before you proceed.

The following are ways to do it:

a. Inspection

* If you are not able to view the container in person, then you must inspect the inside to determine the best way to clean it.

* Grab a flashlight and go inside the container. You might be surprised at how much you find in your initial examination. You might come across pollen, contaminants, stains or dust.

* Look at the corners and surfaces of walls. Don't leave any detail out.

b. Start By Getting Rid Of The Dust

Once the initial examination is complete, it's time to clean out your container. Your containers should be cleaned of dust, dirt, and cobwebs.

A dust mask and goggles are essential for cleaning. This will help you stay safe and protect you from eye or respiratory issues.

* Start at one end of the container. Move to the other side.

c. Make Use of A Leaf Blower

* Although a quick sweep may suffice to remove dust from your home, a leaf compressor or leaf blower might be required to do more thorough cleaning.

* Always be thorough and thoroughly clean all surfaces!

d. Everything needs to be washed

If you keep dust and pollutants away, it's more likely that you'll come across stains and sticky things that won't come off an air compressor. A pressure washer comes in handy here. It is a wise investment to have one.

* Begin at back of container and work your manner to the front.

* Get rid of all stains, including those on walls, floors, or ceilings. Chemicals could cause them.

* Make sure to pay special attention to corners. They tend to gather dust and should be cleaned thoroughly. It is possible that there may be rust on the floor.

High-pressure water can be very useful for cleaning the outside of the container.

Safety glasses are an excellent idea for anyone using a pressure washer, especially when cleaning small areas with limited visibility.

e.

Vinegar works well on very stubborn stains.

* Use vinegar to clean stubborn stains. You can either apply it on the outside of the container or on the inside.

* Let it rest for a few moments before you scrub the stains.

f. Repair Surface Deterioration

While cleaning containers, surface problems such as small holes and dents, or rust can be found.

It's best to address these issues as soon as possible. If nothing is done, the problems will get worse and cause further problems in future.

* You can repair small gaps with a wirebrush. It is very simple and should be completed quickly. You should paint the area where the wire brush was used to clean with rust inhibitor. For larger holes you can cover them by welding a piece of steel to the container.

* It is possible to repair simple rust using white vinegar and a corrosion inhibitor. This can be purchased at any

hardware retailer. You will need to apply the vinegar or the rust inhibitor to the corroded part and then rub it out.

g. Using The Sander

* A sander will make the housing look better and will keep it in great shape for many years. For body parts showing signs of wear, flaking, or peeling, you can use a belt grinder. This will make the container more resistant to the elements and water.

* To protect the machined piece from rust and moisture, paint the surface of the sander with rustproof spray.

* After applying the antirust paint to the container, you can paint both its inside and exterior. High-quality paint lasts for longer.

You can see that cleaning containers not just improves their appearance, but also increases their structural integrity and protects against moisture.

www.ingramcontent.com/pod-product-compliance
Lightning Source LLC
Chambersburg PA
CBHW050409120526
44590CB00015B/1893